GA

The Gate The

CW00430040

The UK Premiere of

STATE OF EMERGENCY

BY FALK RICHTER

TRANSLATED BY DAVID TUSHINGHAM

First performed in the UK at the Gate Theatre, London,
on 6 November 2008

The Gate Theatre's licence to present Falk Richter's play STATE OF EMERGENCY
is granted by arrangement with Rosica Colin Limited, London
in conjunction with S. Fischer Verlag GmbH

Significant Annual Support from

STATE OF EMERGENCY
BY FALK RICHTER

TRANSLATED BY DAVID TUSHINGHAM

Cast

Woman	**Geraldine Alexander**
Man	**Jonathan Cullen**
Boy	**James Lamb**

Director	**Maria Aberg**
Designer	**Naomi Dawson**
Lighting Designer	**Neil Austin**
Sound Designer	**Carolyn Downing**
Video Designer	**Eleni Parousi**
Assistant Director	**Leonie Kubigsteltig**

Production Manager	**Nick Abbott**
Technical Production Assistant	**Peter Jacobs**
Production Electrician	**Chris Porter**
Stage Manager	**Bonnie Morris**
Stage Manager (Rehearsals)	**Liz Kay**
Production Assistant Intern	**Mason Mahoney**

Casting	**Lucy Bevan**
Press	**Clióna Roberts for CRPR** (cliona@crpr.co.uk | 07754 756504)
Production Photographer	**Manuel Harlan**
Rehearsal Photographer	**Bill Knight**

The Gate would like to thank the following people for their help with this production: Sarah Blandy (Senior Lecturer School of Law, University of Leeds), Dan Cheyne, Gareth Fry, Gate Bar, Tom Gibbons, Mark Goddard, Habitat, Kristina Koczian, The Latvian Centre, Thibaut Mills, Nathan Parker, Oliver Rafferty, William Savage.

Production Image © Eric Ngo

Production and Translation Supported by **Goethe-Institut, London**

GOETHE-INSTITUT LONDON

Biographies

Nick Abbott **Production Manager**

Nick is Production and Technical Manager at the Gate Theatre. For the Gate credits include: *Hedda*, *…Sisters*, *Shoot/Get Treasure/Repeat*, *The Internationalist*, *Press*, *I Am Falling* (also Sadler's Wells). Nick was technical Manager at the Chelsea Theatre for *Sacred* and has worked in the Sound Department on various ballets and operas at the Royal Opera House.

Maria Aberg **Director**

Theatre includes, as Director: *Die Kaperer* (Staatstheater Mainz, Germany); *Crime and Punishment* (National Theatre); *Days of Significance* (RSC Swan, US Tour & Tricycle); *Gustav III* (National Theatre, Sweden); *In Foreign Parts*, *Alaska*, *Angry Now* (Royal Court); *Shrieks of Laughter* (Soho); *Stallerhof* (Southwark Playhouse); *Love and Money* (Young Vic Studio); *Duff Luck* (Arcola); *My Best Friend* (Central Space); *A Handful of Dust* (IODC, Cork); *The Maids* (Judi Dench Theatre); *The Lover* (Mountview Studio). As Associate Director: *Pericles*, *The Winter's Tale* (RSC Swan & US Tour). As Assistant Director: *The Crucible* (RSC); *Aristocrats* (National Theatre); *Lucky Dog*, *Sweetest Swing in Baseball*, *The Sugar Syndrome* (Royal Court).

Geraldine Alexander **Woman**

Theatre includes: *Fall* (Traverse); *I Saw Myself* (Wrestling School); *The Maids* (Brighton Festival); *Titus Andronicus*, *A Midsummer Night's Dream*, *The Tempest* (Globe); *Pillars of the Community* (National Theatre); *The Seagull*, *A Woman of No Importance*, *Present Laughter* (Royal Exchange); *The Real Thing* (Tour); *Inconceivable* (West Yorkshire Playhouse); *A Streetcar Named Desire* (Mercury, Colchester); *Private Lives*, *Flesh & Blood*, *Jude The Obscure* (Method & Madness). Television includes: *Silent Witness*, *Extras*, *Feel the Force*, *Love Soup*, *Miss Marple*, *Fatal Passage*, *Coronation Street*, *Taggart*, *Midsomer Murders*, *The Government Inspector*, *Bomber*. Film includes: *The Discovery of Heaven*; *Méchant Garçon*.

Neil Austin **Lighting Designer**

For the Gate credits include: *Ghosts*, *Loves Work*, *Marathon*, *Cuckoos*, *Venecia*, *Une Tempête*. Other theatre includes: *Oedipus*, *Her Naked Skin*, *Afterlife*, *The Emperor Jones*, *Philistines*, *The Man of Mode*, *Thérèse Raquin*, *The Seafarer* (also Broadway), *Henry IV Parts 1 and 2*, *Fix Up*, *The Night Season*, *A Prayer for Owen Meany*, *Further Than the Furthest Thing*, *The Walls* (National Theatre); *Piaf* (also West End), *Parade*, *John Gabriel Borkman*, *Don Juan in Soho*, *Frost/Nixon* (also West End, Broadway & US tour), *The Cryptogram*, *The Wild Duck*, *Caligula*, *After Miss Julie*, *Henry IV*, *World Music*, *The Cosmonaut's Last Message…* (Donmar Warehouse); *King Lear*, *The Seagull*, *Much Ado About Nothing*, *King John*, *Romeo and Juliet*, *Julius Caesar*, *The Two Gentlemen of Verona* (RSC); *The Homecoming*, *Marianne Dreams*, *Dying for It*, *Tom and Viv*, *Romance*, *Macbeth* (Almeida); *Dealer's Choice*, *No Man's Land*, *A Life in the Theatre* (West End).

Lucy Bevan **Casting**

For the Gate credits include: *Hedda*, *The Internationalist*, *I Am Falling*, *The Car Cemetery*, *The Sexual Neuroses of Our Parents*. Other theatre includes: *Camera Obscura* (Almeida); *The Boy Who Fell Into A Book* (English Touring Theatre). Film includes: *Me and Orson Welles*; *The Duchess*; *The Golden Compass*; *St. Trinians*; *The Last Legion*; *Chromophobia*; *The Libertine*.

Jonathan Cullen **Man**

Theatre includes: *Happy Now?*, *Market Boy*, *Albert Speer*, *Ghetto* (National Theatre); *Equus* (Gielgud); *Talking to Terrorists*, *Nightsongs*, *Under the Blue Sky*, *Our Late Night*, *Rafts and Dreams*, *Gibraltar Straight* (Royal Court); *Master and Margarita*, *Nathan the Wise*, *The*

Seagull (Chichester Festival Theatre); *Feelgood* (Garrick); *Our Country's Good* (Young Vic); *Desire Under The Elms* (Shared Experience); *Morning & Evening* (Hampstead); *Venice Preserv'd* (Royal Exchange); *Dr Faustus* (Greenwich); *Chatsky* (Almeida); *'Tis Pity She's A Whore*, *Woman Kill'd with Kindness* (RSC). Television includes: *Poppy Shakespeare* (Film4); *Walter's War* (BBC4); *Ghost Boat* (Yorkshire Television); *Midsomer Murders* (ITV); *Why We Went To War* (Liberty Bell). Film includes: *Fred Clause* (Warner Brothers); *Finding Neverland* (Miramax); *Robin Hood* (20ᵗʰ Century Fox).

Naomi Dawson **Designer**

Naomi trained at Wimbledon School of Art. For the Gate credits include: *...Sisters*, *Mariana Pineda*. Other theatre includes: *Stallerhof*, *Richard III*, *The Cherry Orchard*, *Summer Begins* (Southwark Playhouse); *Speed Death of the Radiant Child* (Drum Theatre, Plymouth); *The Container* (Edinburgh); *Phaedra's Love* (Barbican Pit & Bristol Old Vic); *Different Perspectives* (Contact Theatre, Manchester); *Senora Carrar's Rifles*, *The Pope's Wedding*, *Forest of Thorns* (Young Vic Studio, TPR Productions); *Attempts on Her Life*, *Widows* (BAC); *Venezuela*, *Mud*, *Trash* (Arcola); *Pass the Parcel* (Theatre Royal, Stratford East); *A Thought in Three Parts* (Burton Taylor). Film includes: costume design for the short film *Love After a Fashion*, set design for *Fragile* by Idris Khan. She is also part of artists collective *SpRoUt* recently exhibiting in Galerija SC, Zagreb.

Carolyn Downing **Sound Designer**

For the Gate credits include: *The Internationalist*, *Habitats*, *Under The Curse*. Other theatre includes: *All My Sons* (Schoenfeld Theatre, New York); *Tre Kroner - Gustav III* (Dramaten, Sweden); *Absurdia* (Donmar Warehouse); *Angels in America: Millennium Approaches and Perestroika* (Headlong Theatre); *The Winter's Tale*, *Pericles*, *Days of Significance* (RSC);

Oxford Street, *Alaska* (Royal Court); *Dirty Butterfly* (Young Vic); *Othello* (Salisbury Playhouse); *Moonlight & Magnolias* (Tricycle); *Flight Path* (Out Of Joint); *Topdog/Underdog* (Sheffield Crucible Studio); *A Whistle In The Dark*, *Moonshed* (Royal Exchange); *Hysteria* (Inspector Sands); *Project D: I'm Mediocre* (The Work Theatre Collective); *Arsenic and Old Lace* (Derby Playhouse); *The Water Engine* (Theatre 503 with the Young Vic); *Blood Wedding* (Almeida); *Gone To Earth* (Shared Experience); *Stallerhof*, *A Doll's House*, *The Double Bass*, *The Provoked Wife*, *Mongoose* (Southwark Playhouse); *The Watery Part of the World* (Sound and Fury).

Peter Jacobs **Technical Production Assistant**

Peter studied an HND in Technical Theatre at Northbrook College in 2003. For the Gate credits include: *Hedda*. Other theatre includes: Technical Manager for *Hang Lenny Pope* (Tour); *Wizard of Oz* (Leicester Haymarket); *Grange Park Opera* (2007 & 2008). He has worked as a technician for Thomson Cruise Ships (2008), and freelance for Derby Playhouse and Lichfield Garrick.

Liz Kay **Stage Manager (Rehearsals)**

Liz trained in Stage Management and Technical Theatre at LAMDA. Theatre includes: The Arena Theatre, Wolverhampton; The Alexandra Theatre, Birmingham; The Circus Space, London; The Warehouse Theatre, Croydon; Shakespeare's Globe; The National Theatre; Canadian International Fringe Festival and *Footloose the Musical* (National Tour).

Leonie Kubigsteltig **Assistant Director**

Leonie trained at the Universities of Hildesheim/Bochum, Germany (Drama/Comparative Literature), Northern School of Contemporary Dance (BA Contemporary Dance), and Central School of Speech and Drama

(MA Movement Studies). For the Gate credits include: *The Sexual Neuroses of Our Parents* (Assistant Director). Directing credits include: *You are Blood in My Mouth* (Riley Theatre Leeds); *Stealin' an Arm Ain't No Crime* (Riley Theatre Leeds/Yorkshire Dance Centre Leeds); *The Insect Play* (Shunt Vaults London). As Movement Director credits include: *The Mother's Bones* (M.E.N. Award for Best Performance in a Fringe Production 2006); *The Speculator* (Embassy Studio, Central School of Speech and Drama). Assistant Director credits include: *Studio Plymouth* (Youth Music Theatre UK); *The Beggar's Opera* (Trinity College London/Blackheath Concert Halls); *Long Time Dead* (Paines Plough/Drum Theatre Plymouth). She has recently conducted a research and development project on *Oedipus* (Ted Hughes) and new forms of choric theatre, supported by the Goethe Institute.

James Lamb **Boy**

James is 17 years old. He is currently pursuing a full-time career in acting. Theatre includes: various roles in *Love Bites* (South East tour); Ben in *The Selfish Giant* (The Theatre, Leatherhead); *Disco Inferno* (Secombe Theatre, Sutton). Television includes: *The Bill* (ITV); *Driving Me Mad* (BBC). Film includes: *Heartless* (Richard Raymond Films); *Young Gods* (Crunch Films).

Bonnie Morris **Stage Manager**

Bonnie read Drama at Bristol University and trained in Stage Management and Technical Theatre at LAMDA. She has worked at the Gate since December 2007, having previously stage managed *I Am Falling* and *Hedda*. Other theatre includes: *Angels In America, Faustus* (Headlong Theatre, National Tour); *The Eleventh Capital, Bliss, Relocated* (Royal Court).

Eleni Parousi **Video Designer**

Eleni recently graduated from Camberwell College of Arts. Short films include: *Animi Distentio* (Director), *Under Over The Clouds* (Editor) and *Strata#2* (Assistant Animator). Video design and live performance includes: *EAR* presented at the Royal Albert Hall and Collision Art Festival.

Falk Richter **Writer**

Falk studied theatre direction at Hamburg University. He has worked as a freelance author, translator and director at Deutsches Schauspielhaus Hamburg, Hamburg Staatsoper, Berlin Schaubühne, Düsseldorf Schauspielhaus, Toneelgroep Amsterdam, Burgtheater Vienna, Zürich Schauspielhaus and Seven Stages, Atlanta, USA. Plays include: *Alles. In einer Nacht* (1996); *Kult - Geschichten für eine virtuelle Generation, Gott ist ein DJ* (1998); *Nothing Hurts* (1999); *Peace* (2000); *Electronic City* (2002); *Der Angriff, Sieben Sekunden/ In God We Trust* (2003); *Deutlich Weniger Tote, Unter Eis, Hotel Palestine* (2004); *Eine kurze Verstörung, Die Verstörung* (2005); *Verletzte Jugend* (2006).

David Tushingham **Translator**

David started his career at the National Theatre and has since worked as a dramaturg in Hamburg, Hannover, Stuttgart, Berlin and Vienna. Recent projects include commissioning Simon Stephens' *Pornography* for the Deutsches Schauspielhaus in Hamburg and theatre-rites' *Salt* for the RuhrTriennale. He is currently dramaturg for the performing arts programme of LINZ09 European Capital of Culture. His translations include plays by Falk Richter, Dea Loher, Roland Schimmelpfennig, Rainald Goetz and Rainer Werner Fassbinder.

GATE

"The Gate is our oxygen. It should be on the National Health" *Bill Nighy*

The Gate, London's international theatre in the heart of Notting Hill, is renowned for its inventive use of space and the exceptional artists it attracts. An environment in which artists can create first-class and original theatre, the Gate is a springboard of opportunity, allowing emerging artists to excel and make their mark. With an average audience capacity of seventy, the space has challenged and inspired directors and designers for nearly 30 years, making it famous for being one of the most flexible and transformable spaces in London.

"Great riches in a small space" *Sunday Times*

As joint Artistic Directors, Natalie Abrahami and Carrie Cracknell continue to create international work of the highest standard, which is peerless and provocative, and provides audiences with a unique experience.

"Carrie Cracknell and Natalie Abrahami were still at primary school when Stephen Daldry was running the Gate, but the new joint artistic directors of the tiny but influential Notting Hill theatre may yet have as big an impact on British theatre as Daldry and their predecessors, including David Farr, Mick Gordon, Erica Whyman and Thea Sharrock."

The Guardian

Gate Theatre, 11 Pembridge Road, Notting Hill, London, W11 3HQ
www.gatetheatre.co.uk | Admin 020 7229 5387 | Box Office 020 7229 0706

The Gate Theatre Company is a company limited by guarantee. Registered in England & Wales No. 1495543
Charity No. 280278. Registered address: 11 Pembridge Road, Above the Price Albert Pub, London, W11 3HQ

SUPPORT THE **GATE**

We try to ensure that our creative ambitions are not bound by financial pressures; however, we rely on the generosity of our supporters for almost a third of our income. It is through the generosity of supporters that we continue to break theatrical boundaries.

We need supporters who:

LOVE COMING TO THE GATE

INTRODUCE THEIR FRIENDS TO THE GATE

GIVE GENEROUSLY TO HELP THE GATE

Supporters of the Gate receive benefits such as invitations to a host of events, including exclusive post-show drinks with cast and creative teams, a backstage glimpse of the running of the theatre, regular newsletters and priority booking. Supporters also have the opportunity to develop a close relationship with the Gate Theatre and the team that run it.

The very nature of our tiny venue means that you can see just how significant the support you give is – to our work and the careers of emerging artists.

For more information on the Gate's work and how to support it, please visit www.gatetheatre.co.uk or contact us on 020 7229 5387.

The Gate Theatre would like to thank the following for their continued generous support:

Guardians Emma and Mike Davies, Edward Field, Miles Morland, Jon and NoraLee Sedmak, Hilary and Stuart Williams, Anda and Bill Winters

Keepers Russ and Linda Carr, Lauren Clancy, Robert Devereux and Vanessa Branson, Cory Edelman Moss, David and Alexandra Emmerson, Leslie Feeney, Eric Fellner, Nick Ferguson, David Kaskel and Chris Teano, Tony Mackintosh, Oberon Books, David and Susie Sainsbury, The Ulrich Family

Lovers Anne Braillard, Kay Ellen Consolver and John Storkerson, Charles Cormick, James Fleming, Joachim Fleury, Bill and Stephanie Knight, David and Linda Lakhdhir, David Pike, Kerri Ratcliffe, Kathryn Smith and Ike Udechuku, Sir Tom Stoppard

Special thanks to Jenny Hall

Trusts & Foundations Anonymous, Arts Council England, Earls Court and Olympia Charitable Trust, The Eranda Foundation, Gatsby Charitable Foundation, Jerwood Charitable Foundation, The Mercers' Company, OAK Foundation, The Prince's Foundation for Children & the Arts, Royal Borough of Kensington and Chelsea

Corporate Sponsor Guesthouse West – part of the GuestInvest Corporation

JERWOOD
CHARITABLE FOUNDATION

Jerwood Young Designers at the Gate

Since 2001, the Jerwood Young Designers scheme at the Gate has encouraged the very best of British theatre design, by nurturing emerging designers and celebrating theatre design as an art form in its own right. As one of the most flexible and transformable studio spaces in London, the Gate's small and asymmetrical auditorium has been an inspiration for designers for over 28 years.

The Jerwood Charitable Foundation is dedicated to innovative funding of the arts. Alongside Jerwood Young Designers at the Gate, the JCF supports Jerwood New Playwrights at the Royal Court, Jerwood Young Directors at the Young Vic, producers at Battersea Arts Centre, the Operating Theatre Company, and the James-Menzies Kitchen Award for Young Directors. The JCF also supports Jerwood Opera Writing Programme at Snape Maltings, the Jerwood Awards for Non-Fiction with the Royal Society of Literature Commissions and a number of important projects in the visual and applied arts.

The Gate is grateful for the Jerwood Charitable Foundation's continued generosity and vision for emerging designers, and in particular their support of this season.

www.jerwoodcharitablefoundation.org

STATE OF EMERGENCY

Ausnahmezustand first published in 2004 by Fischer Taschenbuch Verlag in der S. Fischer Verlag GmbH, Frankfurt am Main

This translation first published in 2008 by Oberon Books Ltd
521 Caledonian Road, London N7 9RH
Tel: +44 (0) 20 7607 3637 / Fax: +44 (0) 20 7607 3629
e-mail: info@oberonbooks.com
www.oberonbooks.com

A catalogue record for this book is available from the British Library.

ISBN: 978-1-84002-896-6

Cover photograph by Eric Ngo

Printed in Great Britain
by Marston Book Services Limited, Didcot

Characters

WOMAN

MAN

BOY

WOMAN: Look

MAN: Yes?

WOMAN: Are you alright?

MAN: (*Short pause.*) Yes

WOMAN: …everything's alright, I mean…you?

MAN: What? Yeah, sure

WOMAN: You're…

MAN: What? Yes

WOMAN: Is everything ok with

MAN: With me you mean? Yeah.

WOMAN: You're sure?

MAN: What?

WOMAN: Are you sure?

MAN: Yes

WOMAN: Quite sure

MAN: (*Short pause.*) What? Yes

WOMAN: Uh-huh

MAN: Yes

WOMAN: So there's nothing?

MAN: What? No

WOMAN: Nothing

MAN: What's supposed to be, no

WOMAN: Everything's ok?

MAN: What?

WOMAN: With you?

MAN: Yes

WOMAN: Good

MAN: Yes

WOMAN: Uh-huh

>*Pause.*

>Come here

MAN: What is it?

WOMAN: Just come here

MAN: I'm right next to you

WOMAN: No, come…closer

MAN: Yes

WOMAN: Look at me

MAN: What is it?

WOMAN: Just look at me

>*He does this.*

>What is it?

MAN: What?

WOMAN: What's wrong?

MAN: Leave me

WOMAN: No, look at me

MAN: Yes

WOMAN: That look, something's… I don't know what it is but…something's…

MAN: No it's not

WOMAN: Different

MAN: What?

WOMAN: Different, about you…something's different

MAN: No

WOMAN: There's something different

MAN: About me, no, nothing's different

WOMAN: You sure?

MAN: What?

WOMAN: Are you sure about that?

MAN: Me?

WOMAN: Look at me again

The MAN does it.

Everything's

MAN: What?

WOMAN: Everything's as it should be?

MAN: Yes, of course

WOMAN: Everything's just as it should be?

MAN: Everything's just as it should be

WOMAN: 'S not very convincing the way you say it, say it again

MAN: Everything's fine, everything's just, everything's

WOMAN: I'm worried

MAN: There's no need

WOMAN: I'm worried about you

MAN: Don't be

Short pause.

WOMAN: Can you hear…shooting?

MAN: What?

WOMAN: I thought it had stopped but

Short pause.

no, it's getting closer, every day and I

She stops, a faint noise can be heard, the MAN holds his temples, the WOMAN listens very precisely to the noise.

Shooting.

MAN: No

WOMAN: You can't hear it?

MAN: (*Uncertain.*) No, it's quiet here…isn't it?

WOMAN: Is something burning? Is that something burning?
It's…right here in the neighbourhood, isn't it?

MAN: No

WOMAN: It's getting closer all the time

Short pause, the sound of waves can be heard.

MAN: That's nice

WOMAN: Now they're playing that noise again, that
means that…

MAN: No

WOMAN: Yes, it does, it means…when they play the waves,
then they're doing that so we can't hear the screams, the
gunshots because someone somewhere's gone and tried
again to

MAN: No, people say that but it's not true

Laughs.

They really *are* waves

WOMAN: So where's the sea then?

Short pause.

If they play the sound of waves, then

MAN: They do it because it sounds nice, it's soothing, because it's beautiful, because the sun's going down and it fits...we haven't got a sea, but they'll build us one here soon, it's just a question of money and...whether they get permission to relocate

WOMAN: We're not safe here any more are we?

MAN: Yes we are

WOMAN: At night people get over the walls or somcone's letting them in...someone here in the complex is leaving the gate open at night and

MAN: Shhhh, come on, let's just listen to the waves for a bit and

WOMAN: Look at me

MAN: Yes

WOMAN: Look at my face

MAN: I am

WOMAN: Properly

He looks at her.

It's not you, is it?

MAN: What?

WOMAN: Who's leaving the gate open at night?

MAN: Me?

WOMAN: I'm not sure any more

MAN: Me?

WOMAN: Somebody here, here in the complex, that's what they're saying, somebody…apparently people get in through the sewers or let themselves be thrown in from above, I don't know, that's what they're saying, nobody's saying it officially but…the gun shots, I am not imagining those am I and…at night people go sneaking round the buildings, it didn't used to be like that, can nobody sleep or are they really people from outside, but how are they doing it, how are they getting in here, there's got to be somebody, that's what they're saying, somebody, who… we're not safe here any more…are YOU leaving the gate open? You're not doing that are you? You're not. I don't know… I've been sleeping so badly recently, and the pills, they're…they're not helping, but I… I can't keep on going back asking for more, that… I can't, it would be noticed, there would be talk, then the company would find out and, we're not supposed to be afraid, we aren't, I don't want to be either, I WANT not to be afraid, but…you're…there's something…about

Short pause.

…you and…I'm having such…weird dreams all the time now, I…can see you at night and…but I know… I'm not dreaming, it doesn't feel like a dream because when I wake up and look beside me…you're not there or…no…you're there but you're not you or you're another man who looks like you but isn't you, not like you used to be when…is everything ok with you?

MAN: With me? Yeah

WOMAN: Nothing's changed?

MAN: No

WOMAN: I just thought, because you, it feels

MAN: Calm down, everything's fine

He kisses her.

WOMAN: It's odd

MAN: What is?

WOMAN: You kiss differently

MAN: What?

WOMAN: It's not like you. Something's… different… I don't know, but

MAN: (*Kisses her again.*) Everything's fine, everything's just as it should be, I'm not

WOMAN: Different, but you are

MAN: I'm not

WOMAN: I can tell, something's going on inside you…but what? What exactly is it? Where's my husband? Where is he? I can't find him any more, when I look at you, I

Short pause.

D'you notice that? It's so quiet suddenly, first there's shooting, then the waves and then complete silence, listen…

MAN: It's not shooting, it's kids playing

WOMAN: Uh-huh, so what are they playing then?

MAN: I don't know, they

WOMAN: And why are they hanging from the fence at five in the morning with their eyes wide open? What's that game called?

MAN: I don't know, they're accidents, it happens every now and again, it…

WOMAN: Silence can you hear

MAN: They ought to build a sea then we'd be safe

WOMAN: Then they'll swim across and… I climbed up on the roof yesterday

MAN: You did what?

WOMAN: I climbed up on the roof

MAN: That's not really…on, is it?

WOMAN: It was five in the morning and I looked over at the other side

MAN: Oh yes?

WOMAN: Do you know at night this place is teeming with people

MAN: Teeming?

WOMAN: None of them can sleep, they all walk the streets

MAN: Maybe they're shadows, shadows of the trees

WOMAN: Trees don't run away when you throw stones at them.

MAN: You did…what?

WOMAN: I saw you

MAN: Me?

WOMAN: Yes, you…running around, on the other side, you wanted to get our car out of there but you couldn't find it…you were running round outside the gate, on your own, looking for the car but you didn't find it, it had been torched, all the cars had been torched, and you were looking but the burnt out corpses of the torched cars all looked the same and you'd forgotten where you'd parked it or whether you even HAD parked it, you couldn't remember anything any more, not a thing, you were running around in the dark and you wanted to get back in but you'd forgotten the code and then you ran round in circles between the burning cars and screamed, just screamed

MAN: Uh-huh

WOMAN: And when I woke up you were lying here but I couldn't feel you, you were…still out there with all the dead

MAN: Oh yeah?

WOMAN: We've lost something…is that possible, something's different but it's nothing to do with me, is that right?

MAN: With you?

WOMAN: You're not sleeping

MAN: What?

WOMAN: You're tired but you don't sleep…you lie there next to me and…what's the matter with you?

MAN: What's the matter with YOU?

WOMAN: You know, I… I lie awake at night and… I watch you…sleeping…uncomfortably, you lie awake, all night, tossing back and forth, you pretend to be asleep, you don't want me to notice, you're afraid, lying there, tossing back and forth and

MAN: And what?

WOMAN: What's the matter with you? What's happened?

MAN: Nothing

WOMAN: You scare me

MAN: You scare ME

WOMAN: What are you doing there? What are you looking for out there? Wandering around there, looking and looking, what are you looking for? You stand around the entrance at night for hours on end, not coming in, then you sneak past the guards and

MAN: Me

WOMAN: Something's not right with you, you

Pause.

Are you leaving the gate open at night? Is it you?

MAN: No, I

WOMAN: I listen to you

MAN: You do what?

WOMAN: You talk

MAN: Oh yeah?

WOMAN: In your sleep

MAN: Uh-huh

WOMAN: You talk in your sleep

MAN: Uh-huh

Pause.

WOMAN: What are you talking about?

MAN: What?

WOMAN: WHAT ARE YOU TALKING ABOUT, I WANT
TO KNOW, WHAT?

MAN: What am I talking about then?

WOMAN: DON'T YOU KNOW? Arrgh, something… I can
hear that noise again, I…why are you doing this? Why are
you putting everything at risk? Suddenly now after all these
years we've

Pause, he looks at her.

the way you're looking at me now

Short pause.

that's how you look at me every night

MAN: When?

WOMAN: You wake up for a fraction of a second and look at me, very briefly, like you are now…in panic…like you want to run away… I lie awake…at night…and watch you sleeping, I lie awake and listen to you breathing… I do it every night…night after night… I watch you…your breathing seems to get louder and louder, like a roaring, a screaming, a… I don't know, OWW, I'm so close to you and…where are you trying to run to?…you rock back and forth, sometimes you scream, not for long, YOU SCREAM, don't you realise, you must realise, you suddenly scream, grab hold of me and then… I lie awake watching you because I want to understand, I want to understand but OW this roaring noise, am I the only one who can hear it? I watch you, I watch you sleeping or pretending to sleep, you're dreaming about something, and in your dreams you're wandering around, wandering on the other side of the fence, talking to the people there, getting lost behind the rubbish tips, lying down in the snow and laughing, you're lying there with your eyes closed and laughing…such a strange…laugh…it's coming out of you…at night…and you're talking, talking in your sleep… where…where are you? where are you then? at night? where are you then? where? that's what I want to know, where?

MAN: I'm with right you

WOMAN: No

MAN: I am totally and utterly with you, I…what am I supposed to… I mean, where…what?

WOMAN: You hold onto me and scream… I want to give you everything you need, but…what am I supposed to do, I…where's my husband gone, where is he? What have you done with him? WHERE IS HE? I WANT MY HUSBAND BACK, what have you done with him, where is he, where?

MAN: (*Cautiously.*) I am here

WOMAN: No

MAN: Yes, I'm

WOMAN: No, you're not, you are not, that is not…and that is why I thought

MAN: What?

WOMAN: I thought that…it would be better if…it might be better

MAN: No

WOMAN: Better if I

MAN: No

WOMAN: Purely to help you I mean, if I, if I…if I were to tell them

MAN: No

WOMAN: So that they could check

MAN: What? No

WOMAN: Check to see if everything's alright with you

MAN: No

WOMAN: It might be something chemical…your magnesium levels aren't right, there's something…your blood levels or… I just thought, maybe

MAN: No, my levels are fine.

WOMAN: And you've had them tested?

MAN: Yes

WOMAN: Have you?

MAN: Yes

Short pause.

WOMAN: What about more sport?

MAN: What about it?

WOMAN: Didn't you have to do more sport?

MAN: Me?

WOMAN: Get out in the evenings, go for a walk round the lake with the dog.

Short pause.

MAN: We haven't got a dog

WOMAN: Then we'll hire one, you can hire things like that here, or we'll order one, then

MAN: No, I don't want a dog.

WOMAN: Or you could dig in the garden with the neighbours

MAN: That's…there are people employed to do that…that's not planned, for us to go round digging up the garden, if everyone did that, then

WOMAN: Hold me tight

MAN: What?

WOMAN: Hold me tight, please

MAN: (*Hugs her for a while.*) Is that good?

Short pause.

WOMAN: We can tell each other everything, we don't need to keep any secrets from one another, do we? We don't need to

MAN: No

WOMAN: If something wasn't right then we would tell each other, wouldn't we?

MAN: Yes

WOMAN: If a time comes when you don't want to have sex with me, you just don't fancy me, then…you don't have to

MAN: But I want to, I mean, I like doing that, so, I…

WOMAN: Yes?

MAN: No, that's…fine, that's what we agreed, once a fortnight

WOMAN: You don't have to if it's too much bother.

MAN: But it's not too much bother, I mean, it's…no, once a fortnight…

We need that too, I mean, we…you do too, don't you?

WOMAN: It's ok if you miss the odd one, honestly…take a break and… I can do without it for a month or two, that's fine… I mean…there are people who NEVER

MAN: Stop it

WOMAN: They just come home and stare at the ceiling

Short pause.

Compared with that what we've got here is beautiful, desirable, enviable… I mean there are people who just lie around and shout all day or bang their heads on the ceiling or THEY KEEP wanking, wanking and wanking and wanking till they're so empty and wrung out they reach a state of stupidity where they keep running into the door without ever finding a way out, THEY DO IT OVER AND OVER AGAIN, by those standards we've got a great life, haven't we, eh?

The MAN has closed his eyes as if he's gone to sleep, he tries to breathe evenly.

Darling.

Short pause.

Love.

Short pause, very tender.

I understand, other couples don't have sex, we work...we do a lot of work, so...so we don't always have to have sex with each other

The MAN says nothing.

I think it's ok for you to come home and not want to talk to me, if you just sit down and don't look at me, don't touch me...don't talk to me

MAN: But I do

WOMAN: You don't notice

MAN: I

WOMAN: 'Cause you're not here

MAN: I

WOMAN: On some endlessly long sheet of ice somewhere... somewhere in the Arctic a group of young polar bears are searching for food...suddenly the ice breaks and they all plunge down three thousand metres into the depths and drown...you can hear their screams for days while they're drowning, while the sun slowly eats away their brains

Pause.

That was on tv yesterday.

MAN: A documentary?

WOMAN: On the news.

Pause.

Look...it's ok, if you don't think about me or...my body, sure, I mean I understand... I am over 40...and by that time your body

MAN: Stop it

WOMAN: No, no, I understand, I understand...my body's

Rather forced laughter.

27

And yours, well, yours is

She strokes his body, takes a close look at a couple of places and laughs.

It gets to be like that eventually, it's not a bad thing, we'll deal with it, you know, course we will

Pause.

It's just, it's just…you don't have to be happy with me, and you don't have to make me happy, that's ok, I really don't have such high…in that area but…you should…

Short pause.

…go to work

MAN: What?

WOMAN: Because if you don't do that…if you show the same kind of attitude there as you do here, then

MAN: Me? No, how

WOMAN: I just think you ought to go back

MAN: But I'm there

WOMAN: Your body's there

MAN: What?

WOMAN: You're not present and…they can tell…there's something missing…you're no fun.

Pause.

It's alright, if you find that somewhere else, not here, not with me, after all this time no one's expecting a lot of action in that department, that's fine, but…but, can I say this one thing, as a 'friend' or whatever you want to call it: get yourself what you need to keep on working, get it…so you…so…you've got to work, you've got to be good, you understand what I mean?

MAN: Yes

WOMAN: They rang up

MAN: Uh-huh

WOMAN: They rang me up and asked about you

MAN: Did they?

WOMAN: Whether everything's alright, they're worried, they're all really worried about you.

MAN: Really?

WOMAN: Yes, all of them, the management, the team, the lot

MAN: Uh-huh

WOMAN: They're all really worried about you…and about me, they're asking how I can have let this happen that you, let you become so different, you're so absent, they want to know where you get to in this absence of yours, what you're thinking, they're asking me for clues because none of them can make any sense of your behaviour, it's so unusual, like something happened…they…they've asked me, not to leave you to your own devices, to take responsibility

MAN: Uh-huh

WOMAN: You're so passive

MAN: But I

WOMAN: You're getting left behind

MAN: No

WOMAN: You're not achieving

MAN: What, of course, I

WOMAN: Your performance is down

MAN: No

WOMAN: That's what they're saying

MAN: That's not true, I'm doing everything just like I…like I always do

WOMAN: But something's different

MAN: No

WOMAN: Your performance is down, they've measured it

MAN: That can't be true

WOMAN: It is

MAN: No

WOMAN: And they want to know why

MAN: I do everything they way I've always, I get just as much done as before

WOMAN: But you're not enjoying it

Short pause.

It's no fun any more, you've fallen out of love…with the job and that's…they can tell and they're wondering why, because the job's still the same so it would seem to be something with you

MAN: I do enjoy it

WOMAN: And they want to know what can be done

MAN: I enjoy doing it

WOMAN: They've had a couple of meetings about it with the team, individual interviews and…and here in the complex, they've talked to the neighbours…they've looked at your video analysis, all your stats for the last fifteen years.

Short pause.

MAN: What?

WOMAN: They say you hardly laugh any more, you…don't enjoy the job any more, you do the work…hesitantly and look out of the window a lot, three or four minutes an hour on average. And increasing.

Short pause.

What are you looking for?

MAN: I

WOMAN: The others don't like to be in the same room as you, late at night you seem…tired…you're always the last one to leave the office but what are you doing there? Your scores are falling…what are you doing there so late if you're not working, what? When you all go away at weekends or just go out for a drink together…no one wants to sit next to you, when they put together new teams, nobody wants you on their team, nobody, you don't really engage in conversations…it's like it's not really you who's talking, it's like you're…somewhere else…and the clients can tell, the clients…the clients don't want appointments with you, you've got fewer appointments

MAN: That is not

WOMAN: 3.45 per cent less than last month

Pause.

4.13 per cent less than the month before, you're dropping back, soon…soon you won't exist any more, the numbers…are against you…you don't convince the clients any more, because…because…what is it? What's wrong, what?

Pause.

…like you're…somewhere else and where you are exactly that's something they'd like to know…they really want to know that.

(*Pause, very softly.*) Where are you?

(*Short pause, normal volume.*) You don't tell jokes any more, you used to really enjoy telling jokes, why don't you do it any more?

MAN: (*Uncertain.*) I do

WOMAN: (*Produces a piece of paper with diagrams on it and checks.*) 17 per cent down on last month. 23 per cent down on the same month last year.

MAN: I

WOMAN: You'd tell people about yourself, your life, stories, anecdotes, or if there was something you'd enjoyed in one of the shows you'd act it out, imitating the candidates or someone stumbling…they'd all laugh, they thought it was…funny…it cheered them up, gave them so much strength they really wanted to be with you, get through the day together with you, but…why not, why don't you do that any more?

MAN: But I

WOMAN: No

MAN: I

WOMAN: Tell me a joke then

MAN: What? No

WOMAN: Come on

MAN: Now?

WOMAN: Yes

Long pause, he starts but breaks off after the first word.

MAN: This man goes into

Breaks off, short pause.

This

WOMAN: And you'd sing

MAN: What?

WOMAN: Before you used to…sing when you were at work and…now you don't any more

MAN: Yes I

WOMAN: Sing then

MAN: No

WOMAN: Sing

MAN: Now?

WOMAN: Yes

The MAN hums something softly, then stops.

MAN: I

WOMAN: Come on, let's sing together

MAN: Leave me

WOMAN: No, come on, let's practice

MAN: Leave me alone, can't we go…and eat or something

WOMAN: (*Starts singing.*) I want to live

Waits for him to sing the second line and when he doesn't she carries on singing.

I want to give

Waits for him.

Come on.

MAN: I've been a miner for a heart of gold

WOMAN: You missed several awaydays, where were you?

MAN: I was there

WOMAN: No you weren't

MAN: Why do you believe that?

WOMAN: I KNOW, they called me, they… I know. (*She flicks through a series of papers.*) I know all about it, for God's sake, have you any idea what you're doing… I'm going to have to leave here too if you…you can't do it any more, if you can't get into the next round…they'll…they've got out all your files, gone through them all again, your aptitude tests, they thought you might have cheated, you had very consistent results, absolutely top results and now, if it carries on like this, they'll

MAN: I do my best

WOMAN: That's not you any more, I don't know you any more, that's not my husband, that's some other man, you're not the man I…maybe it would be better if you

MAN: No

WOMAN: Or I, if we, if we're not going to, but

MAN: No

WOMAN: What's the point of all this?

MAN: No

WOMAN: Go to sleep

MAN: I'm trying to

WOMAN: Get some sleep, rest, find whatever it is that you… find it, that I don't know, that strength, find it, go on… Don't lie awake, sleep

MAN: That's what I'm trying to do, I'm…

WOMAN: What are you talking about in your sleep?

MAN: Me, nothing

WOMAN: I listen to you

Short pause.

I write it down

MAN: You do what?

WOMAN: I write it down, I... I...make notes, I...asked Stefan whether

MAN: (*Like a word in a foreign language.*) 'Stefan'?

WOMAN: Your friend, you go back a long way, I thought maybe he could

MAN: I've known him six months

WOMAN: But you're with him all the time

MAN: We sit opposite each other in the office

WOMAN: Yes, but you

MAN: Occasionally we go and do...sport together, but

WOMAN: I thought maybe he can help you, but

MAN: What are you doing?

WOMAN: I'm worried about you, I don't want people to think I don't look after you, you know, I don't want people to say that I neglected...they asked me to

MAN: Who are you?

WOMAN: They like you, we all like you, we don't want to lose you

Short pause.

You seem upset

MAN: Is there anyone else here in this room?

WOMAN: You seem upset?

MAN: Is anybody there?

WOMAN: You seem upset, right now this minute, now... the way you're...yes, now...the way you're looking at me

MAN: What way?

WOMAN: So tired

MAN: Me?

WOMAN: So exhausted

MAN: Uh-huh

WOMAN: Is it anything to do with me?

The MAN does not answer.

Is something annoying you?

MAN: No

WOMAN: About me?

MAN: No

WOMAN: Do you fancy me?

MAN: What? Yeah

WOMAN: Say it

MAN: I fancy you

WOMAN: Doesn't sound very convincing

MAN: What?

WOMAN: It doesn't sound very convincing the way you say that, say it again

MAN: Now?

WOMAN: Yes

MAN: Is there someone else in here with us?

WOMAN: Say it

MAN: What is this about?

WOMAN: Say it

MAN: Can't

WOMAN: What?

MAN: Can't just because you tell me to

WOMAN: Say it

MAN: NO

WOMAN: SAY IT DAMN IT SAY IT

MAN: I fancy you

Pause, she laughs, the sound of waves.

D'you like the new stove?

WOMAN: 'S nice

MAN: It is nice, isn't it

WOMAN: Yes

MAN: It's calming.

WOMAN: Adds value

MAN: Maybe you should look at it a bit more often.

WOMAN: We'll get a better price later on when we come to sell

MAN: Maybe you should just sit in front of it a bit more often
and take a good, long look at it, at the fire, at the way
the flames slowly build up and then die away again…a
very long look…a very, very long look…maybe then
everything'll sort itself out.

Pause.

Leave me alone all of you

WOMAN: Right now I wouldn't if I were you…

MAN: Shut your stupid, just shut your idiotic

WOMAN: Not now I wouldn't, no, that

MAN: I'm doing what I can

WOMAN: If that's all you can do then I'm very

MAN: I'm doing everything I can.

Short pause.

WOMAN: He was screaming again

MAN: I know, I'm not deaf.

WOMAN: Is it actually him or?

MAN: Did the police come again?

WOMAN: No, it was his coach.

MAN: Which one?

WOMAN: The co-ordination coach

MAN: Is he sleeping?

WOMAN: He'll have an hour, then he wakes up again, last night there was some kind of noise, footsteps, then he spent two hours in the shower with all that horrible loud shouting and crying the whole time and then they played that violin concerto through the streetlamps again and it was so loud that…waves, the sound of waves all the time…the next morning there's the charred remains of a dog lying in our drive and the boy's wearing his jacket and trainers in bed, he's all out of breath…and when I open the door he shouts at me LEAVE ME ALONE JUST LEAVE ME ALONE

Short pause.

Two hours later I go in anyway, he's lying awake, breathing heavily, I go in there, he doesn't even know I'm there, I sit down on the edge of the bed, he's rocking and rocking, cradling his laptop in his arms like it's a teddy bear, very carefully I try to touch him, to calm him down, suddenly he tenses up and twitches…twitches and twitches…and then his eyes open wide and he shouts GET OUT OF HERE THE LOT OF YOU RIGHT NOW

The MAN has fallen asleep.

Hello.

The MAN does not react.

Darling.

(*As if she's talking to some undefined person in the room.*) You can take him away now

MAN: (*Opens his eyes immediately.*) What?

WOMAN: (*Laughs.*) See, I still know how to get your attention

Laughs.

If we don't do something, we're going to lose him.

MAN: He's sixteen, boys at that age…

WOMAN: He's thirteen. He's got a plan, he's got some kind of plan, but I can't work out what it is, I can't work it out.

MAN: Maybe you've

WOMAN: I hid yesterday. Under his bed and he

MAN: You did what?

WOMAN: I was hiding under his bed last night and he

Short pause.

he's odd, our boy, I don't know, somehow…he touched my hand and then he said, don't worry Mum, I'll get rid of him.

MAN: You were lying under his bed while he touched your hand?

WOMAN: He meant you.

MAN: How can you

WOMAN: I can feel it, he's up to something. With YOU. There was a photo of you under his bed. But it wasn't you in the photo, it was just something that looked like you, something that reminded me of you but…he was shaking when he

She breaks off.

Short pause.

MAN: Maybe you just dreamt it all.

WOMAN: What do you mean, 'it all'?

MAN: It all.

WOMAN: 'It all'?

MAN: I mean, maybe…

WOMAN: In my dream there was water running the whole time, it went on for hours, it was boiling hot and our son was standing in the shower screaming and screaming and screaming while our dog was out in the garden bleeding to death in the snow

MAN: We haven't got a dog

WOMAN: And then this morning the charred remains of a dog were lying in our drive and its guts and its severed head were outside our bedroom window and our bathroom was flooded.

MAN: I didn't see anything.

WOMAN: The day before he stared at me for a whole hour and then he said 'Know who you are'.

MAN: He's going through a difficult

WOMAN: He doesn't speak in sentences, he

MAN: Of course

WOMAN: No he doesn't, he doesn't

MAN: Of course, he goes to school doesn't he

WOMAN: (*Laughs.*) Yeah, right, they're starting to bring in
teachers from the other side now because they're running
out of money because OUR HUSBANDS aren't bringing
enough money home because their returns are down
because they'd rather look out of the window or fall asleep
than…that's why my son can't talk properly, all he can
speak is…gibberish that… I can't understand a word of it, I

MAN: You've just got to listen properly

WOMAN: There's nothing to listen to. Most of the time he
doesn't say anything at all.

MAN: What does the co-ordination coach say?

WOMAN: Wait and see

MAN: Uh-huh

WOMAN: The man comes here five times a week, walks off
with a ton of money every month and says 'Wait and see',
that's all he says, BUT I DON'T WANT TO WAIT AND
SEE I'VE DONE ENOUGH WAITING, what's wrong
with our boy? What's wrong with him? I can't get to the
bottom of it, he doesn't write anything, nothing, no diaries,
nothing, not even notes in the margins of his schoolbooks,
his emails are all completely average, his internet use,
the sites he visits, who he chats to, who he orders things
from or what films he rents, the coach says it's all perfectly
normal, that can't be true, it can't, that boy is not normal,
I can tell, he keeps such irregular hours, there's something
there, something's not right, something's not right about

The MAN has fallen asleep again.

*The WOMAN watches her husband sleeping, she looks around her,
rushes round the room then she goes right up close to her husband
and looks at him sleeping.*

They feel you might be 'ill', you've got to get well again,
take yourself out of circulation for a while, to think about
your self, life, everything…how you want to spend the

time, that's what they said, 'the time you've got left', because it seems you can't go on like this.

Pause.

What are you DOING? What? Do you know how long it's taken us to get this far? To get this house, your job, this property here in the complex, where everyone wants to be and there are hardly any places left, to get a school for the boy at last, to sleep through the night at last, where it's quiet, there are trees, avenues, short distances, not travelling through the city for hours every morning, missing the train, assuming it's actually working, stuck in the car somewhere for hours on end, never getting where you want to go, always in a rush, always frustrated, it's so quiet here, we've got our own airport here, we're picked up in the morning, taken to where we need to go, there are people here who have the same interests as us, people who look out for us, people who are glad to be living here with us, who organize garden parties for us, play badminton with us. If it's our wedding anniversary, the whole community has a party, the children go off to school in the morning and get there, they walk home in the evening and get here too, where else does that happen? And if we've got to work late or go away for the weekend, there are places where we can leave them and where they'll stay until we collect them. There are no muggings, no crazy old people who can't stop asking you the way because they've lost all sense of direction, they've escaped from their homes or they've not got a home to go to anymore, throwing themselves in front of moving cars, here nobody throws themselves out of a window out of desperation, here nobody shouts at their wives or beats their children, ties their children to a radiator at Christmas and abandons them till they've starved to death, the lake, the sunset here, the silence

MAN: What silence? You said yourself that you…

WOMAN: There are piles of applications and loads of competent people, there have never been as many competent people in the world as there are now and they all want to come here.

MAN: We hardly know anyone here. We get up while it's still dark and go to work. We don't get back until long after the sun's gone down. We have a garden, a park, a little lake next door, yes, it is nice here, nice and quiet, EXCEPT FOR THE SHOOTING AT NIGHT… We've got no friends here. Sure, we go to all these get-togethers and barbecues and garage sales and polo nights and garden parties and weddings and I don't know what other events and training seminars and theatre productions and beauty contests and wellness conferences and what do I know parenting counselling and coaching seminars and then for a change we do yoga or pilates, we've even got a creative writing group, where we all get together and write short stories

Laughs.

but…we don't know any of them, we hardly talk to them, not properly, we all exchange the same sort of pleasantries and no one gets any closer, nobody's remotely interested, nobody's interested in anything, even when they're all singing and laughing together and telling jokes and WHAT DO I KNOW acting out funny scenes from the shows, nobody's seriously interested in these painting lessons or creative writing or church services…or we get a surfing weekend as a bonus but we can't go because we've got to work or we've got community service, we've got to attend all these meetings here, or meetings at the town hall where no one ever says anything of any consequence or because we're just too stressed to get through all the security checks or because we don't know how to surf in the first place, because we don't enjoy it, the whole ocean's already full of surfers, all members of some bloody team who are surfing away all their bonus points, so as not to stick out or to go windsurfing from some hot air boat

WOMAN: You're mad

She drinks.

MAN: And every Saturday we go to the shows and watch some load of people they've brought in from the sticks in buses beating the crap out of each other, we watch them at the weekend and laugh ourselves sick but we're afraid of them, we're afraid, we hope they're not going to stay here, that one of them isn't going to hide under a bus and find a way in here before they leave and attack us all, none of our old friends has managed to get into the community here, they're all still outside the gates and can't get in or don't want to get in, do you never think about them? Not ever? Or we spend hours in the market square standing waving after parades of soft toys or whatever, what are our neighbours called? What are their names? Tell me, tell me, WHAT ARE THEIR NAMES? Here in our CELEBRATION COMMUNITY, what is it we're actually celebrating? 'Cause I don't know any more.

WOMAN: They all queue up by four thirty in the morning and rattle the gates, they want to get in, they all want to get in and they're no better and no worse than you, but they've got the right ATTITUDE, d'you understand, they have a laugh. And they sing. They enjoy themselves, their lives and the world around them, they LOVE their families AND their jobs, they leave the house in the morning in a good mood and come back in the evening in a good mood, then they go and do some sport with their friends and at night they sleep in a good mood with their wives. Men who enjoy a good fuck, you understand, they're waiting out there and they want your job and to be honest I've got nothing against it if they

MAN: Be quiet! The boy can hear us.

WOMAN: Let him

MAN: Afterwards he'll tell everyone at school again how coarse and stupid his mother is.

WOMAN: Shush

Short pause.

Perhaps he is listening

Short pause.

MAN: They all gave us such weird looks at the last parents' evening, as if they knew exactly what we talk about in the evenings.

WOMAN: He's so odd, he scares me.

MAN: Shh, was that? No I think…is he even at home?

WOMAN: I don't know.

Pause.

(*Speaks quietly.*) There's no prison here and that's why, they say, it would be better to suspend your contract for a while.

MAN: They said that?

WOMAN: Yes, 'suspend your contract for a while'… I hope you know what that means…no one's going to sack you

Short pause.

You get a lot of time to retrain.

She laughs.

A lot of time to prepare for another career, as whatever. Maybe you can start guarding the gate from next Friday or scraping the bodies off the electric fence of all the nutters who try to climb over here.

She fetches herself a drink, opens a bottle of wine and drinks.

MAN: I

WOMAN: What's wrong with you, I'm so frightened, I…
I don't know you any more, what are you doing, do you know what you're doing?

MAN: Please, I, it's just that

WOMAN: You're gambling with our lives, our futures.

Pause.

If they suspend the contract for a while, we'll have to move out of the house, we'll have to leave the complex, the lake, the garden, last week someone had to leave and within 72 hours somebody else had taken their place and nobody says anything about it, you understand, they're gone, simply gone, we'll have to leave the community, the company, go to another city, more interviews, aptitude tests, for days, questionnaires, do we fit in with the other residents, where have we come from, what's our background, are we team players, how do we handle stress, then they'll question the boy and put him through a load of behavioural tests and apart from all that… DO YOU KNOW HOW OLD WE ARE? Nobody's going to take us in our mid forties, why?

She laughs.

This damned container

She means her body.

nobody wants it any more

She laughs.

You can become a dustman or scrub graffiti off the walls or guard the railway station or I don't know… Lie down in the snow and hope someone dumps you in front of the clinic, we'll lose everything

MAN: (*Pause, he considers for a moment, then.*) What? What are we going to lose? What?

WOMAN: EVERYTHING

MAN: What?

Short pause.

What 'everything'? Just what 'everything' are you talking about?

Short pause.

WOMAN: His emails are entirely normal and yet he spends all night sitting in front of the computer and the next morning none of the security cameras work, they transmit images of people who are meant to be, but no, they show some kind of weird stuff going on on the other side…how does he get those pictures?

Short pause.

That dead dog's still there in the snow.

MAN: What?

WOMAN: They promised it wasn't going to snow here any more

MAN: Did you tell them?

WOMAN: The dead cat's still hanging in the tree. He just lies there in his room with headphones on, perfectly quiet, with his eyes closed and tonight, when we're trying to sleep, then he'll be ghosting through the house

MAN: Did you tell them to take the dog away.

WOMAN: And the way he…the stuff he wears…and always alone, he's always alone, but the coach says that's perfectly alright. Can't we send him on some kind of course?

MAN: What kind of course?

WOMAN: I don't know but there must be something, some kind of course that can raise his self-awareness, relieve him of stress or…you know, sometimes I dream about white surfaces. White people moving very slowly across these white surfaces and talking to each other in very simple sentences, saying things like:

– I love you

47

– I know

– I like everything about you

– I like everything about you too

– The most beautiful moment for me is to wake up next to you and know you're there and you always will be

– That's just what I feel

– I love you

– I love you too

And these white people slowly wander round this white surface and there's snow falling and their hearts get warmer and warmer the colder it gets outside and they hold hands really tight

MAN: And suddenly the ice breaks and they all plunge down three thousand metres and drown…you can hear their screams for years while the sun slowly eats away their brains.

WOMAN: Just like you.

MAN: Yes, just like you.

Short pause.

How did your amateur dramatics at the Community Centre go?

WOMAN: The director cut one of my lines

MAN: Uh-huh

WOMAN: You're not doing us any favours there

MAN: Is that what you said to him

WOMAN: No, my husband, that's what I said to my husband

MAN: Uh-huh

WOMAN: Now I don't any more

MAN: What?

WOMAN: Everyone else got to keep their lines

MAN: Maybe there were artistic reasons

WOMAN: No, it was pure spite, he hates me, just like everyone else in the group

MAN: I don't believe that

WOMAN: Everyone else got to keep their lines, just not me

MAN: Maybe he was trying…

WOMAN: You're not doing us any favours there

MAN: Just to

WOMAN: I've spent weeks practising that line

MAN: The rhythm

WOMAN: Then suddenly without any warning

MAN: Maybe the rhythm

WOMAN: The line's gone

MAN: One line here or there

WOMAN: That line was essential to my character

MAN: So there were characters?

WOMAN: I needed that line

MAN: Were they historical?

WOMAN: That line meant everything to me, without that one line I was… I was invisible, I wasn't there any more YOU'RE NOT DOING US ANY FAVOURS THERE I wanted that line, without that line I

MAN: So what did you say?

WOMAN: You're not doing us any favours there

MAN: No, I mean

WOMAN: Yes, what do you mean? You're not even listening. You're not doing us any favours there.

MAN: To him, the director?

WOMAN: Oh I don't bother talking to him, he just laughs when you say something to him, he wants everything to be jolly, that's all.

MAN: Yes, but

WOMAN: Nothing, I didn't say anything else, I said: if I'm not allowed to say this line then I'm not going to say any of the others either, I WON'T SAY ANYTHING ANY MORE, that's what I told him, he can ring me if he changes his mind, my character needs that line, it doesn't need any of the others but it needs that one, that one, you understand, otherwise it can't breathe, it's going to suffocate, its throat is going to freeze shut and it's going to throw up everything it's eaten in the last few years in one hard, slimy icy lump and stir it around in its own disfigured mask of a face burnt out by the emptiness of its own utter talentless uselessness like a bucket of paint you pour onto a blank canvas and stir around for so long that eventually it turns into a WORK OF ART, I NEED THAT LINE and if I don't get that line then nobody should say anything, we don't need words any more because humanity will be finished ONCE AND FOR ALL, there'll be no more people any more, at least not any who can put one foot in front of the other without the benefit of artificial limbs or very strong painkillers, THEN THEY'LL ALL COLLAPSE, if there's anything left that's worth leaving the house for, then it'll all be gone, EVERYTHING, if I lose that line the world will lose its light and GOD WILL RECLAIM THE GIFTS HE HAS WASTED ON THE UNWORTHY

MAN: What's the play about?

WOMAN: The truth

MAN: And what else?

WOMAN: It's about the truth – for my character it's only ever
been about the truth although all the others claim the
opposite, but they're wrong, the others are wrong, I'm
right, they're wrong, it's a play about a woman who is right
and about other people who are wrong, RIGHT YOU
UNDERSTAND I AM RIGHT RIGHT, that's what the
play's about

Short pause.

and it's really up to me to decide what lines I need and
what I don't need.

MAN: Are you still going to do it?

WOMAN: Everyone else got to keep their lines, some of them
even got new ones, just me, I was the only one who's got a
line less, the only one who had their tongue cut out in front
of all the others and was turned into a figure of ridicule, I
was the only one who got chained naked to the gates of the
prison and paraded on a long leash and everyone killed
themselves laughing KILLED THEMSELVES YOU
HEAR ME KILLED THEMSELVES and my line was the
only line that really needs to be heard, you can get rid of
any other line in the play just NOT THAT ONE

(*Suddenly dangerous and aggressive on a level never suspected
before.*) NOT THAT ONE YOU UNDERSTAND NOT
THAT ONE IT'S MINE just like my child he's mine too
and I'm not going to let anyone or anything take him away
from me! D'YOU UNDERSTAND ME YOU... VICTIM

MAN: What?

WOMAN: I'm not going to let my son be taken away, I'm not
going to move from here either, I'm not giving him up,
he's mine, he's going to protect me when they all come
over here, when they break through the walls, when they
swim over here and set fire to everything, line us all up
and stare at us...for hours...staring and staring...their

knackered, awkward, filthy eyes staring at us for days, for hours on end, and we'll just stand there in a line naked and they'll be staring at us for days on end till we collapse devoid of strength or will and they'll just leave us lying there, step over us while they settle down in our homes and watch the fire in the grate and listen to the gentle roll of the sea on a balmy summer evening, because there will only be balmy summer evenings, of absolute calm and purity, like a song from long-forgotten days, bright and tender and somewhere in the rising flames a child is playing… I don't care about the theatre group from the community centre. I don't care whether I say that line or not…but they will come and their stares will overwhelm us and we will drown in a pool of blood created by all the questions they have for us when they line us all up and we're called to account for everything we've done…they're going to really fuck us ragged with their big dirty bodies till we've nothing more to say, NOTHING, it's going to be so quiet here, so quiet, and all that, all that pent up testosterone over there's going to flush us away, we'll be out of here, gone.

MAN: You're sick.

WOMAN: I can see the truth

MAN: Your mind is completely sick

WOMAN: I went there

MAN: When?

WOMAN: Last night. I had a look round

MAN: Uh-huh

WOMAN: I was there, first time in years, walked down our old street, where we both went to school, when there still were schools and streets, I had a walk around, at night, took a good look at everything, MAKE AN EFFORT WORK, I don't want to lose all this

MAN: We were happy there

WOMAN: That was twenty years ago, WORK MAKE AN EFFORT, if they suspend your contract then…this house belongs to the company…they'll just book a lorry, it'll take fifteen minutes, no more, they've got special units, twenty minutes at the most, and every trace will be wiped out, we won't exist here any more and we'll never see the boy again

MAN: How did you get through the gate at night?

WOMAN: I don't want to go back there again, I want to stay here, in this area if the police come they DON'T shoot you…where else does that happen? Where else have you got the feeling that the police are genuinely there for your safety, they won't rape you while you're out shopping, where else does that happen? Not even the camera crews go there any more, all images are embargoed, no photos, nothing's permitted, and you've got no chance of ever getting out of there again, no matter how many forms you fill in, even if you fill the forms in correctly you're not going to get out because there aren't any places left in the centre, if we have to leave now, if we have to leave now then…then we'll never be coming back, I'm telling you, never ever, we will be out for ever and stay there…with all the confused, deranged filth the rejects

Short pause.

Sometimes you can hear screams at night, sirens, you can see fires on the other side, in the Autumn, when the leaves have fallen, in November: then through the bare branches you can see the city behind the electric fence slowly falling apart. The people there, demented, ugly, full of anger and incomprehension, muddling their way around between all the billboards, all the hospitals closed, the schools

MAN: I love you

WOMAN: That's not the point.

MAN: I can't do this any more

WOMAN: That doesn't matter. Nobody can. Pull yourself together, everyone else is.

MAN: I've got the feeling…

WOMAN: 'Feeling', 'feeling', that's not the point. People like us ought to be glad that we've made it this far, we shouldn't really be here, we don't belong and they notice, they notice that…they notice that you don't enjoy anything any more and they see it as ingratitude, they've given you so much, given you a job, gradually built you up and you thank them with this indifference, this inertia, nothing matters to you.

MAN: Come here

WOMAN: No

MAN: Come to me

WOMAN: No

Sound of waves.

We're going to see this through to the end, together, you and me.

MAN: And where exactly is that going to take us?

WOMAN: To the end, till we can't go any further, till we've no strength left.

Pause.

D'you understand.

MAN: But I don't

WOMAN: Do you understand!

MAN: Yes.

The BOY enters.

WOMAN: Hello

The BOY says nothing, looks at his parents contemptuously and crosses the space in the direction of his room. The MAN and WOMAN say nothing, they sit there waiting, motionless.

BOY: (*Comes back.*) You shouldn't

WOMAN: Hello, how are you?

BOY: Thousand times. A THOUSAND TIMES MAN

WOMAN: Would you like something to eat?

BOY: How many more? I MEAN HOW MANY MORE?

He exits again.

Pause.

The BOY enters once more.

NO FUCK NOT NO I YOU OH MAN

He exits, re-enters, intending to leave the house, looks at his mother.

I'm warning you

He exits again.

WOMAN: Stop.

BOY: What do you want?

WOMAN: I wanted

BOY: What? What is it you want?

WOMAN: Sit down

BOY: No

WOMAN: (*Very softly.*) Just sit down

BOY: No

WOMAN: Please just sit down

BOY: No, I

WOMAN: Sit down, just for a moment

BOY: If you're going to…then

WOMAN: Please just sit down a moment, ok

BOY sits down, stares at the WOMAN and the MAN I'm sitting

I

BOY: Can I go now?

WOMAN: In a minute. I wanted to

Breaks off.

Pause, the BOY stares at her again, looks deep into her eyes.

BOY: 'S everything ok?

WOMAN: What?

BOY: With you?

WOMAN: I

BOY: 'Mum'

Pause.

WOMAN: I wanted to

BOY: Yeah?

WOMAN: Listen, I

BOY: What?

WOMAN: I wanted

BOY: Yes?

WOMAN: To ask you

BOY: What?

WOMAN: Something

BOY: What is the

Short pause.

matter with you. 'Mum'

WOMAN: Just a minute.

Pause.

Are you moving the furniture in the night?

BOY: What?

WOMAN: Are you

Short pause.

The furniture. Every morning it's always

Short pause.

Somewhere else

Short pause.

Here, I mean. In the room. Every morning the furniture is somewhere else in the room and I can hear scratching, this scratching sound, in the night, and you never sleep.

BOY: Can I go now?

WOMAN: You walk around the house. Slowly. Or you crawl. During the night you crawl around the house on all floors and rearrange the furniture. Some things are missing and the paint...the paint's been scratched off the walls.

BOY: Can I go now?

WOMAN: Where are you going?

BOY: OUT!!!

MAN: (*Has woken up.*) How did the training go?

BOY: Can I go now, please.

WOMAN: No.

MAN: Come on. How did the training go?

BOY: God's sake, it's training, that's all, we chase the ball around and try to score goals, what about it, what the hell, can I go now?

WOMAN: No, first I want. At night…where are you?

BOY: I'm tired

MAN: He's tired.

WOMAN: Of course he's tired, he never sleeps.

BOY: Can you lend me some money, I need

MAN: How much?

BOY: Two thousand

MAN: Two thousand?

BOY: Yeah, I…please

WOMAN: Two THOUSAND?

BOY: Yeah, it's only because…just give it to me

WOMAN: Where are you?

BOY: Here

WOMAN: At night, where are you then?

BOY: Here. In my bed.

MAN: Do you know anything about those boys who are missing?

BOY: Leave me alone.

WOMAN: Do you know them?

BOY: No one knows anything about the missing boys.

WOMAN: But you know them?

BOY: Can I go now?

WOMAN: You meet them occasionally?

BOY: What?

MAN: Do you

BOY: CAN I GO NOW?

WOMAN: Where do you want to go?

BOY: Out.

WOMAN: Yes, but where

BOY: OUT I WANT TO GO OUT

WOMAN: YES BUT WHERE?

BOY: (*Calm again.*) You know, out, God's sake, out.
JUST OUT.

WOMAN: You sleep less than four hours a day.

BOY: I want to get out of here.

He stands up and goes to the door.

MAN: Yeah, go on, go, just go, go out

WOMAN: No, you're staying here. Sit down there.

Short pause.

Do you know the boys who were found on the fence? Do
you know them?

The BOY looks at the floor, does not answer.

Did you know them?

BOY: How am I supposed to know?

MAN: Did you know them?

BOY: What does he mean?

WOMAN: Did you know the boys they found on the fence?

BOY: How am I supposed to know that. They didn't have faces
any more, no idea if I knew them or not.

MAN: But a couple of boys disappeared at the same time, what about them, did you? I mean do you know

BOY: I don't know anything

WOMAN: Why aren't you sleeping? What are you doing all night?

He sits down, a DVD can been seen in his pocket which could not be seen before.

What's that film you've got there?

BOY: Don't know. Some film.

WOMAN: Oh right.

MAN: What your mother means is what's on there.

BOY: Don't know. Don't know it.

WOMAN: Where did you get it from?

BOY: Don't know, someone gave it to me.

WOMAN: Someone gave it to you, fine.

Short pause.

Who?

BOY: What?

MAN: Who gave you the film?

BOY: Kid in my class.

WOMAN: What's this kid's name, do we know him?

BOY: No.

MAN: Name.

BOY: Thomas.

WOMAN: Aha, Thomas, and what does this Thomas do.

BOY: He's in my class.

MAN: Yes, and what does he do apart from that, when he's not at school. What does he do then?

BOY: Homework or he goes on the computer.

At the word 'computer' the MAN and WOMAN exchange alarmed glances.

MAN: What's this film about? What's the story? Has it got a subject?

WOMAN: We're only asking.

BOY: But I don't know the answer. Can I go now?

WOMAN: No, we're talking now, we're having a conversation. For God's sake, what's so difficult about that, we can just talk to each other, can't we, we're a family.

BOY: But I don't know this man.

WOMAN: Stop being so stupid, that's your father, so

BOY: So what, I still don't know him.

MAN: Let's just talk for a bit then

Pause, no one says anything.

How was it at school?

BOY: It's Sunday.

MAN: Ah right.

Pause.

WOMAN: Well... Paul? Do you still see him now and again?

Pause.

BOY: D'you mean me?

WOMAN: Yes I mean you, who else would I mean?

BOY: Your husband.

WOMAN: No, I mean you.

BOY: Who's Paul?

WOMAN: You know, Paul.

BOY: Don't know any Paul.

MAN: Your friend Paul from the Astronomy Club.

BOY: What Astronomy Club?

WOMAN: For God's sake, the Astronomy Club. The one you started six months ago.

BOY: You sure you've not got me confused with somebody else?

WOMAN: No, I mean YOU.

BOY: Some other kid who lived here some time

WOMAN: No

BOY: Or from another marriage with another husband, is that possible?

WOMAN: You started an Astronomy Club and there was a boy in it called Paul.

Pause.

BOY: Paul?

WOMAN: Yes, Paul.

BOY: Oh right. You mean Paul.

WOMAN: Yes, that's right, Paul.

BOY: He disappeared.

WOMAN: Disappeared, how?

BOY: Gone. Suddenly he just wasn't there.

WOMAN: And why is that, because…look, I'm only asking because

The MAN has fallen asleep.

BOY: Can he go?

WOMAN: What?

BOY: Don't want him here.

WOMAN: You didn't sleep again last night.

BOY: I did

WOMAN: No

BOY: I did

WOMAN: You weren't in your room.

BOY: You shouldn't go looking in my

WOMAN: Where were you?

BOY: Leave me alone.

The MAN wakes up.

MAN: Leave him alone. Just leave him alone.

WOMAN: What's that DVD got on it?

BOY: A film

The MAN has fallen asleep again.

Why don't you send him away, we don't need him.

WOMAN: Are you letting those people in here at night?

BOY: All he does is sleep. He doesn't do anything, he just lies around. WHO IS HE ANYWAY?

WOMAN: Answer me: are you letting people in here at night?

MAN: Leave the boy a

BOY: You keep out of it.

MAN: But you're the one I want to

BOY: But I don't want you to

WOMAN: QUIET! There are people in here who don't belong here

BOY: Go

MAN: What?

BOY: Go away, please, just go.

WOMAN: What do you know about it?

BOY: (*Stands up.*) HE'S GOT TO GO

MAN: All sick

WOMAN: The cameras don't work any more, someone's hacked into them, the recordings have all vanished, the CCTV cameras don't transmit any more, they send nonsense, things that aren't happening.

MAN: Your mother's spent all day evaluating the CCTV footage and doesn't know any more whether she dreamt it all or whether

WOMAN: QUIET! The cameras are showing something that's not happening. And that scares me! They send weird, really, really weird, have you got something to do with this?

BOY: Can I go, I've got to

WOMAN: NO! Where is this Paul? He was here, he used to keep visiting you, where is he now? HE WAS ON ONE OF THESE FILMS, why are the cameras showing him here at night when he's disappeared? Where is he? What are you doing at night?

BOY: You're sick, both of you.

MAN: You are

BOY: What

MAN: You're sick, everyone says so!

BOY: Who says that?

MAN: Everyone

BOY: Who's everyone, who?

MAN: Everyone.

BOY: Yeah, who, who says that?

MAN: EVERYONE

WOMAN: What are you doing on your computer at night, what is it?

BOY: Everyone talks about you.

WOMAN: The CCTV pictures show…people who aren't listed anywhere and nobody knows whether these people actually exist or whether

MAN: Everyone talks about YOU. My son is…peculiar, inhibited, no one can get near him. He's up to something.

BOY: He should leave me alone. Tell him to go back to sleep AND LEAVE ME ALONE. If you come into my room once more, at night, and search through my things or mess up my data, then YOU ARE OUT OF IT, got that. It happens very fast.

Pause.

WOMAN: What is going ON here? MY GOD!

Pause, sound of waves.

BOY: Can I go and play now, Mum?

MAN: 'Go and play', what is it you want to play?

WOMAN: They found a child's body near the town hall last night, someone had thrown it over the fence, was that you?

BOY: There is no town hall here.

WOMAN: BUT THAT'S WHAT THE CAMERAS
SHOWED.

BOY: Bollocks.

WOMAN: All the cars were torched, that's what the cameras
showed, but the next morning…they were all there
again…all new cars, so we'd have no suspicions, or were
they never torched, because they were just images that
YOU during the night while you're not sleeping and you're
here next door on your computer

BOY: I've got to go

WOMAN: Where?

BOY: To my friends.

MAN: You haven't got any friends, they've all disappeared.

WOMAN: (*To the BOY.*) Do you know the code? Did he give
you the code? That gate has got to stay shut, even if you
don't understand that yet, but that gate has got to stay shut.
There are all those young men there on the other side
and you, you're all alone, one little boy on his own in the
whole area and there, there are hundreds, thousands, tens
of thousands in every high rise, you haven't got a chance
boy, when they come, they're going to trample right over
you, they won't even see you and that's why we've got the
code, THE FENCE HAS GOT TO STAY SHUT, DO
YOU UNDERSTAND ME!

She grabs hold of the BOY.

DO YOU UNDERSTAND?

Short pause.

BOY: YES!

She releases him, short pause.

Can we move away from here, Mum?

WOMAN: Where do you want to go to?

BOY: There's nothing here.

WOMAN: There's everything here we need for a wonderful life.

BOY: If I see one more happy pensioner painting the sun setting over the sea, I am going to beat them to a pulp.

WOMAN: We've got our own airport

BOY: But we don't fly anywhere.

WOMAN: Why should we when we've got everything here?

BOY: We hardly know anyone here.

WOMAN: We know everyone here, absolutely everyone.

BOY: I don't mean that, I mean

WOMAN: And everyone knows us

BOY: But still, there's…nothing here, nothing.

He looks at the MAN, lying there with his eyes closed.

And this bloke here, 'your husband'.

WOMAN: Come here

BOY: Couldn't you find any other father for me? Did you have to pick him? Was there nothing better on offer? There are masses of men looking for families, why did it have to be him? He's useless.

WOMAN: Come over to me, please

BOY: Who is that?

WOMAN: Come on!

Takes him in her arms.

You mustn't destroy your own future. One day you'll understand the point of all this.

Short pause.

The gate has got to stay locked, that is the one really important thing I can tell you to take on your way, don't forget that, ever: the gate has got to stay locked!

Short pause.

BOY: Can I go out for a bit, just a bit, please. Can I just go out for a bit, please, can I. Listen to the waves. Hear them breaking, the sound, the colours of the shadows in the evening sun. The roar. The light at the other end of the water. The sound when they're just about to break, it's so… beautiful.

Pause, he exits, pause.

MAN: (*Wakes up.*) Has he gone?

WOMAN: He knows something.

MAN: He's not coming back.

WOMAN: Maybe he is the one who's leaving the gate, but how can he be, he doesn't know the code, the kids don't know the code, do they? Did you tell him the code, did you?

MAN: They've all vanished. Unreachable.

WOMAN: You don't care at all

MAN: Go to sleep

He closes his eyes.

WOMAN: Talk to him.

MAN: He'll just laugh at me.

WOMAN: Try somehow

MAN: He despises me

WOMAN: Everything's leaving me, everything.

MAN: Go to sleep.

WOMAN: Everything's swimming away. The tide's coming in and it'll wash them up on the shore and carry everything else away. There'll be nothing else left, nothing.

Pause.

You've got to find it again, inside you, that or else we're or else we'll have to NO you've got to, that strength, you've got to go there and you've got to, you've got to look for it, look inside yourself, keep going, the boy needs you, the boy's completely confused because you, these children are all leaving us, they've all gone, quite suddenly, they go out and never come…you've got to, can't you see how confused our boy's been since he could feel that we're, we're no longer secure here, that we might have to, because you, they tell the children at school if their parents have problems at work, if their performance dips, can't you see how CONFUSED the boy is, you've got to

MAN: (*With his eyes closed.*) Perhaps he knows everything, he knows the code and lets them in, just to, to see what they're going to do, like other boys his age dissect insects and watch them slowly die, twitching and writhing in pain, so he, as soon as he's cracked the code, 'll open the gate and let them all in, to see how we're slowly buried under the tide of them, how they slowly cut off our air supply, how we, you and I, and everyone he knows slowly twitch to our deaths.

Pause.

They shot them.

WOMAN: What?

MAN: They shot Paul and the other boys, I heard, it's what they're saying, because they wanted to open the gate at night, just to see what would happen and it'll be exactly the same with him…he won't be able to stand it here much longer and then he'll try to break through the fence and open the gate

WOMAN: That's your fault, he can tell that there's something not right with YOU and he's reacting to it, he's very… vulnerable

MAN: (*Still with his eyes closed.*) What do you think about us?

WOMAN: About us?

MAN: Yes. About you and me, our life? Do you like it?

WOMAN: Yes.

MAN: Are you sure?

WOMAN: We've got everything here we

MAN: No, I mean you don't miss anything?

WOMAN: No

MAN: You've got no

WOMAN: Needs, no

MAN: You want everything to

WOMAN: Where we are in life…for people like us… remember where we've come from, it can't get any better for us, it can't, it can only get worse, it's all in your hands

MAN: I work

WOMAN: You don't enjoy it

MAN: I

WOMAN: You don't love your work, you go in but you're not looking forward to it, to the people there, your desk, your computer, you're not looking forward to that, you don't love them, the people you see there

MAN: They're different every day

WOMAN: That doesn't matter, you've got to love them

MAN: The others just disappear

WOMAN: And you don't love them and that's something…
they notice…like him…they notice that something's
different, it doesn't matter that you're still good you're
committed, they notice that something about you…IN
you…has changed and that's…not what they want… please

MAN: What?

WOMAN: Please

MAN: What is it?

WOMAN: Please please please

MAN: What is it?

A wave is heard.

WOMAN: Now

MAN: No

WOMAN: Yes

MAN: No

WOMAN: Gunfire, can you hear it? Now he's gone.

MAN: I can't hear anything

WOMAN: Now, this second, and…now they're playing those
waves again, I…

MAN: People just say that…they really are waves…believe me

WOMAN: (*Pause, wave gets louder.*) You've got to get it back

MAN: What?

WOMAN: Inside you, you've got to

MAN: He's not coming back.

WOMAN: You've got to, got to find it again

MAN: That's how they all disappeared.

WOMAN: Or else we'll be lost, no matter how hard you work, they can tell, they can feel it and I can't go on lying for you any more

MAN: Or he'll make it, he'll meet the boys who've disappeared and they'll open the gates together and watch us slowly plunge to our deaths, thousands of metres, our legs twitching in mid-air as if they're trying to touch the ground and we're screaming, screaming as the sun slowly eats away our brains. You can't do WHAT?

WOMAN: I've got to tell them tomorrow whether you want to stay here or not, whether you want to try again or whether they should give the place to someone else, another man who wants to make more of his life than you, I'm supposed to tell them that tomorrow.

MAN: When?

WOMAN: (*Looks at her watch.*) In eighteen hours

Short pause.

Look for it, look for it inside yourself, for that, that, look, you're so inert, you're going to kill us, you've got to find it again and… find it and keep it, hold it tight and…if they give someone else your contract, we're both dead, then we'll be living a life that's not a life any more.

MAN: And this one here, is this one?

WOMAN: I don't know, yes, it is, yes, this here, this here is the best thing that people like us can get, people with our background, we can't expect any more, we've made it, we can't get any higher, don't gamble with this, please, don't throw this away, go to sleep, doesn't matter how, go to sleep, have a really good sleep tonight and go in there in the morning with new strength, go to sleep and find that… that joy, find it again at last, or else we're finished.

Fade out. The End.